Static Flow

A Collection of Poetry, Writings, and Photos

By
Tyler Max Redding

With Foreword By
Lj Redding

And Special Contribution By
Evelyn Lowell Prieto

Featuring Afterword of Selected Poems by James B. Rice,
Late Father of the Author

Copyright ©2024 by Latent Press LLC for Tyler Max Redding.
Copyright ©2024 by Latent Press LLC for James B. Rice.
Copyright ©2024 by Latent Press LLC for Evelyn Lowell Prieto.
Copyright ©2024 by Latent Press LLC for Lacia Anniya Redding.

All rights reserved.
No portion of this book may be reproduced in any form without written permission from the publisher, except as permitted by U.S. copyright law.

This publication is solely based on the personal experiences of the author. Any resemblance to any person(s) living or dead is coincidence.

This publication covers what some would consider "dark" theming. Please keep in mind, this is a work of art based off events in the author's life. In no way do the publisher or author advocate self-harm or the harming of others. If you are feeling desperate, please seek professional help in whichever way you feel is right for you. Just hold on. Love yourself.

Neither the author nor publisher condone the use of illicit substances. If you are struggling with addiction, please seek professional help.

You should consult with a professional when appropriate. Neither the publisher nor the author shall be liable for any personal or commercial damages, including but not limited to special, incidental, consequential, or other damages.

Book Cover by Tyler Max Redding
Illustrations by Tyler Max Redding
Proofing by Lj Redding
First edition 2024
ISBN: 979-8-9894509-4-7

For Mom—You knew *me* before I was even born; it was your unconditional love that led me home.

Table of Contents

Foreword by Lj Redding	8
No Ordinary Preface	10
Fight or Flight	

Spring
Currencies	14
Eclipse	15
It Is What It Is	15
A Great Man	16
Magic Stick	18
Convergence	19
Make the Time	20

Summer
Let's BE	24
Stay OUTSIDE the Lines	24
Phoenix Feathers	25
They Called Her Moppet	25
Beautiful Pain	26
Catalyst	27
Goodbye, C	27
I Am Not the Sea	28
Where There's a Will	29
Stardust Lovers Sonnet	30

Autumn
Withstand	34
Seasons	34
Take the Wheel	34
Ashes of Grace	35

Embers	35
Burn	36
I Just Want To Live	36
Never	37
Triggered	37
Crests	38

Winter

Umbrellas	43
The Battle	44
Evermore	45
What Gives?	45
Murder Of a Crow	45
Eye of the Storm	46
Flow State	47
Whiplash	47
Tamed Heart	48
The Force of Flow	48
Grammie	50

The Rising

Frequencies	54
Vessels	55
Splash	55
Florida	55
Bang the Drums	59
Co-written with Evelyn Lowell Prieto	59
Every One Hundred Years	60
The War Is Over	62
Transcendence	65
"Once More, With Feeling…"	70
Journal Entry	2 - 4 April, 2024	

Extended Photo Section   78

About the Author　　　　　　　　　　　　　98

Afterword—

Selected Poems of My Father: James B. Rice

Introduction　　　　　　　　　　　　　　102
Poetry by James B. Rice
Friends　　　　　　　　　　　　　　　　　105
A Lesson　　　　　　　　　　　　　　　　106
Life　　　　　　　　　　　　　　　　　　107
Well Done　　　　　　　　　　　　　　　108
Family　　　　　　　　　　　　　　　　　109
A Simple Lesson　　　　　　　　　　　　　111
A Short Story　　　　　　　　　　　　　　112
Felix　　　　　　　　　　　　　　　　　　113
Apple Juice　　　　　　　　　　　　　　　114
What is a Friend?　　　　　　　　　　　　115
The White Dove　　　　　　　　　　　　　117
A Picture From a Memory　　　　　　　　　119

Dedications
Henson Family—In Loving Memory Of:　　122
Henson Family—In Loving Honour Of:　　**123**
Rice Family—In Loving Memory Of:　　　　126
Rice Family—In Loving Honour Of:　　　　127
Redding Family—In Loving Honour Of:　　128
Redding Family—In Loving Memory Of:　　128

Special Thanks To:　　　　　　　　　130

Foreword by Lj Redding

Heal your trauma, people, because if just one little piece of it can do all this? Then I'm going to be INVINCIBLE by the time I'm through.

The views are spectacular.

— Summer of 2023 I wrote something pertaining to my own trauma that ended in the above text. Reading that back now, after witnessing Tyler's personal healing journey and subsequent growth only serves to reaffirm the sentiment. I've watched him burn, hotter than the sun, only to all but extinguish his own flame, and then, burn even harder. Over and over, around and around …

… until he figured out for himself that he's an inextinguishable light, perpetually aflame. His own intensity comes from a place of love—for all of us and for himself. Tyler has worked so hard, to be in a place where he can truly, (in his own words as you'll see!) look into his own soul and fully feel all there is, and still come out on the other side. Because it's darkness that cannot withstand him, rather than the other way around.

He's light—a blazing inferno—to be in his presence is to feel safety, empowerment and inspiration. Healing is within your—my, and all of our—reach.

I hope the pages before you will ignite *your* fire, because once we're each on the other side of our personal hell, there'll be no room for darkness in heaven. (*Inspired by Tyler's line, "I walked into heaven by walking through hell.")

No Ordinary Preface

Fight or Flight

Such madness—
Coming down from scraping catastrophe,
Chronic fight or flight—
I walked this earth with guns to both—
My head and heart—for years,
Like any second a bomb could've gone off;
And that battle's over—a near-miss tragedy,
Turned Divine comedy,
Thankfully, gratefully—
I'm still here,
But there's no quantification of words—
I could put through your ear,
To describe the shock, this feeling,
Now that my blood is free of chemicals—
I'm reeling, trying to catch up—
Like, YES, my dad's really gone,
As so many others,
I'm learning I need to let go on levels—
I wasn't able with weapons aimed,
At my heart,
Just HOW is this ALL really real?
And how am I still here?
So many plights, overlapping—
Night after night—years upon years—
MY GOD, how they burn;
I know one thing, those angels of mine—
They deserve a medal,
For working so much overtime,
I burned through my life,
As if there was a knife, at my very throat,

A hundred thousand miles—quite literally,
Bears, wolves, cliffs, and ice—
Freaking five hundred milligrams—
Night after night—for real, yes!
And let's not forget—
That final TWENTY-ONE milligram magic shroom trip!
Just how on EARTH, am I still on EARTH?!
Pointless, so needless—to analyze, I know,
I'm just REELING, from turbulence—
A thousand miles an hour—
To near-absolute stillness;
And all within this time, on Earth,
As chaos closes in, as we spiral up and in,
Just—DAMN!
Still, I wouldn't change anything,
It all brought me to NOW—
A second chance, life can finally begin;
Grateful to the ones who stayed,
To the ones who walked away—
I say goodbye, with love—I forgive—
But I'll never trust you again,
Let any other traitors in this midst fall away;
I go to war—NOW—not to fight, but to heal,
I bow to the Divine WITHIN, and NEVER to any other—
EVER again;
This chess board will BURN,
This collective will WIN!
LOVE, it is, it's all that remains—
It's in every cell of my being,
It's every memory, every pain—
Pain is what saved me—having courage to face it,
Only by the Grace of LOVE go I—

For now, I ride out this comedown,
Fight or flight will melt away,
As a hurricane—dissipating over the ocean,
There's absolutely no fight I can't win,
For now, I just breathe,
Release the tears, absolve the grief.

Welcome, to Static Flow.

Open your mind, open your heart, and take it all in. This was written with *love*, I hope you enjoy it.

Spring

The traveler had ascended the highest peaks, or so he thought.

Currencies

Energy of currency:
We say don't say that we hate money—
Money is energy, wavelengthed authority,
Can be used so darkly;
Sure, it's all intention—but shouldn't we check our own excesses?
Energy of freedom, for me, just please;
But still can't tell me why these words matter here,
Even as they flow from wells,
I don't get it, words aren't spells—
Even as I'm casting them,
Outcasting—blasting languages, for ages—
If tones cause wavelengths that hypnotize heart-aches,
With fifty million languages—
Every sound with infinite meanings,
How then, do your third dimensional words even KNOW what you mean?
Oh right—INTENTION!
Gotta zoom back out now, words can get so heavy now—
All I know is this—I can't handle much more—
Of this turbulence,
I'm burning within,
Intentionally;
Perhaps SOUL is also a spectrum, in itself;
Let currencies flow...

Eclipse

Eclipse rising—
Cruising tides,
Raising bridges to eliminate divides;
Madness—what turbulence,
Almost scares me back into fences,
But no—I've let go—
Bending not breaking,
Rising at the fall of the flow.

It Is What It Is

It is what it is—
Such a simple phrase,
My mom and I made our own,
As my dad slowly faded away;
Some people would get triggered,
"He's dying! Can't you see?"
Thinking we were trivializing—
What would inevitably come to be;
OF COURSE we knew—
Did they not know—the fortitude—
It took to watch him slowly go?
We weren't making light of it—
We simply knew accepting it—
Was the only way through;
You can't run from loss,
Loss is part of life—
If you love them on the mountaintops,
Then you walk them through the valleys;
Try denial all you want,

But someday you'll find out—
Grief—suppressed—will finish you,
If you don't get it off your chest;
Feel it—FEEL IT ALL!
Every drop of sorrow—all the pain,
Of course it hurts, but you won't learn,
If you just run away.
It is what it is—true for anything,
Even for the most painful things,
That every life will bring;
It's not making light—it's SHEDDING light,
Just ACCEPT what you can't change.

A Great Man

I remember clearly,
A day in March last spring,
I was out exercising,
Mom texted "CALL ME NOW!"
I knew the second I heard her breathing—
On the other line—
Something bad was happening,
I knew it all too well.
There'd been an accident,
Uncle Tommy wouldn't make it out.
I dropped to my knees—right there—
On Kissimmee Trail Bridge,
No—just no—not again—
This can't keep happening;
By some miracle of Heaven,
Auntie Candy walked away,
Nobody could explain just how,

But I know our angels—
Had wrapped their arms around her that day;
We'd all endured so much loss,
Such a big family, ties and bonds—
It does come at a cost.
Yet another funeral reception—
Down in Fellowship Hall,
I couldn't stop the memories—
And I know I wasn't alone.
But in the end, all this loss,
I know brought us all closer—
Memories echo through the years,
But there's bonds that can't be broken;
I feel so very lucky,
To have known a man like him,
Grew up right across the street,
He was always there to lend a hand;
Even as a child, he spoke to me—
As an equal—
Something most adults don't do,
We shared so many tastes in music,
Was always there to fix my bike too,
But he'd also make me learn—
How to fix it for myself.
I wish it hadn't ended like that,
But it is what it is,
I'm grateful beyond measure—
Auntie Candy is still with us.
I'll love and miss you always,
Until we meet again,
I'll honour you, just like the rest—
With every step I take.

Magic Stick

I saw ghosts, in that smoke—
Like demons, coming for me,
Join us, they said—
Inviting me in,
Smoke in the truck,
Fogging my thoughts,
Aftermath of the night's terrible plot;
And every day forward,
I'd drive cross the canyon,
Turning that corner,
To the sight of that ominous blue sea,
Inviting me, calling me in—
"I'll swallow you whole—
You won't feel a thing!"
I've still yet to understand,
How I managed to resist, to withstand—
All of that pain, trauma and fears—
Without surrendering to those waves,
Giving my life away,
Perhaps part of me did die out there—
Because I'm still here,
I still know and hear the call of those waves,
But I have been saved,
Only by the grace and mercy—
I was able to show to myself,
I walked into heaven by walking through hell.

Convergence

Convergence—
Of everything,
In the most beautiful way—
Every narrative will fall away,
No more lines,
Zero confines—
Left to imprison,
No more division;
I see an end in sight—
A new beginning,
A rising of all which once was—
And shall be again—
Only far beyond anything—
Anyone from this age could imagine;
Interdependence—
No gates of fences,
No judgement of form,
Inhibitions reformed—
Melted away,
With everyone loved,
And everyone stays,
Only the NOW,
Only a ONE,
Committed to all—
Obligated to none.
So, open on up,
Set free your soul—
If you define yourself with lines,
You only imprison your mind—
Open up, join us,
Come on up—
We're waiting,
Arms open with love.

Make the Time

Just a plant, seemingly like any other; its bold colours catch the eye of a passer-by.
"Oh how pretty", as he moves along.
He's so busy and caught up in the tireless drudging of everyday life, there's no time to stop and observe further.
"No daddy, look!"
The little girl grabbed her dad's hand and dragged him closer to the flower.
"See! It's like a little city!"
The dad kneeled down to take it all in: the fully opened petals, new buds just beginning to open, even the tiny, prickled blossoms up and down every stem. There were the tiniest of insects coming and going, some carrying away pieces of leaf and petal the plant had dispatched. An entire little ecosystem lay before him, teeming with life.
Something moved nearby, they looked up to see a rabbit snacking on another plant.
"Why's the bunny eating the flower? It's so pretty!"
"I think because he has to eat something baby, doesn't he. It seems everyone right here just helps each other out."
"Why can't people do that?"
"Some do, baby. But I guess most of them are just so wrapped up in things, they tend to overlook the simple. It's not their fault."
"I guess you have to go to work now, right?"
"Not today, baby. We're gonna hang out right here."
The little girl smiled. It was a good day.

Make time for the quiet, the plain. Take it all in—
the worlds within worlds all around. Some of the
most seemingly complex things in life melt into
lucidity, if we only pause to observe.

Summer

The traveler moved through space and time like a god.

Let's BE

Can't we just BE?
Come breathe with me,
Who dared tell you there isn't time?
Just open your eyes,
There's so much more—far beyond the limits we've been sold,
An infinite vastness to explore;
Just BE with me, just breathe,
Feel that sun, the breeze,
The warmth and love from earth and trees...

Stay OUTSIDE the Lines

Who decides where the lines go?
Who even knows,
Why do we even need lines at all?
Are you really comfortable conforming—
To everything that goes against your soul?
Who told you what colour to be in your soul,
Or who to love,
Or what to wear?
How to conform to the perfect hair,
If that's your thing—great,
But if not—
It's never too late—to shatter those molds, refuse those lines,
There is exactly NOBODY who has any right to keep you confined!

Phoenix Feathers

Pondering what it is to burn,
What it is to rise from ash—
To return—
To the One of self, of former—
To NOW, I AM, in all its glory;
Chaos spreads, yes, no doubt—
Just remember, some lights NEVER go out!

They Called Her Moppet

Sweet angel lady,
With ringlets for hair,
She loved her flowers and gardens—
Many a hummingbird there;
Not the easiest life—
Compared to some we know,
You'd never know it, to talk to her,
She made the best of it all;
I remember Christmas parties,
She'd be "Santa's helper"—
Passing out the gifts, as well as hugs—
One could never feel so loved—
As when she'd wrap her arms around you,
A safe harbour of infinite love;
My graduation party—
A few too many drinks,
She snatched a red tablecloth—
Wrapped it like a cape!
She was a superwoman,
The life force of the party,

She'd dance and twirl so joyously—
Was hard to not be affected—
By a light just so Divine,
An angel in human form—
Who walked this very earth;
She's an angel—even now—
She watches over us all.
I'll never see a hummingbird,
Without thinking of her smile,
And the kindness that she showed to me—
In most difficult of times;
Her spirit was unmatched,
And we could all learn from her—
When life throws you lemons—
Forget that lemonade—
Just throw a freaking party!

-I love you eternally, sweet lady.

Beautiful Pain

Freshly healed wounds sting ever so sweetly,
Beautifully—
A beautiful pain, slow-burning on repeat;
Eclipsing heartaches—
Turning hells to heavens, it's alchemy.
That's it—nothing left to speak on it,
And I know in my mind—I won't play repeat it,
It was what it was,
Beautiful and dangerous—
A sunburn for the ages.

Catalyst

Jagged ends are just treacherous paths to new beginnings,
Who is anyone to judge the truth of one who only dwells within?
What a lesson, when you saw it coming but kept on going—
Then again—
Who am I to judge?
I saw myself crashing and still went jumping;
Shattered pieces rise from ashes—
And I wish that catalyst—
Had been anyone, but *you*.

Goodbye, C

This grief isn't shadows,
It's like an eclipse,
Another near-miss,
Just another loss—within a loss,
The greatest of all,
Like I'm losing you all over again,
She was my last connection—to you,
The pain that started it all,
And maybe that's just a cycle completing,
I've walked too far to ever return,
That's why I know inside—
This was always meant to be part of my ride,
I just need to watch it burn,
I'm just so tired—
As strong as I am, I'm not immune to pain,

The deeper my roots to hell,
The further to heaven I'll rise,
All the more light to shine.

I Am Not the Sea

Some bonds can be bent, not broken—
Tiring, the seas of unspoken,
Exhausted lies—unfolding,
Untold—before my very eyes,
Can't scream free, just see—
These visions—they unravel in my mind,
Matter, labels, goods and evils—
These aren't visions!
How is this not division?!
And to make rhymes worse,
My entire LIFE—
This entire VERSE—
It's one big collision—
Of a single cell imploding on itself;
If the whole point of this dimension—
Is union—reunion—
Then why's my timeline like a funeral—
For hellos?
Why come,
To divide what was already ONE?
So, I run,
Even to tiring, unspoken seas—
They'll never need me to be—
ANYTHING—
But what I AM, you see.

Where There's a Will

Where there's a will, there's a way,
Such an inflammatory thing to say—
To the ear of the beholder,
The one in the throes of inner war;
But—WHAT a promise,
Even when your ears are deaf to it,
It rings true—will is ENTIRELY up to you,
Even in the darkest hours,
Even as you can't draw breath from air—
That promise is still there;
You can make a choice,
You can use your voice,
Even if you can't speak—just go within,
You'll learn nothing is impossible—
With or without reason;
There's no battle you can't survive,
If you can find the will within,
There's not a fight that you can't win.

Stardust Lovers Sonnet

Long ago, lovers divided stardust,
Time and space became linear and bound,
Awakening asleep, physical thrust,
A cosmic wheel turned them round and round.
Life after life, sailing seas of sworn lust,
Each other searching cinema of sound,
Select cycles reuniting in just,
Until seas and sands left them lost around.
Adrift through currents of cycle's distrust,
Like magnets, slowly attracting each round,
One became a sea, other ship of rust,
Ship sailing sea's glistening, golden sound,
Sea woke to ship, as ship to sea in trust,
In love, oceans swallowed beautiful sound.

Autumn

Relapses and resurfacings—could the traveler surrender?

Withstand

I burn as the sun,
Like before—
Before and again—
Inverted heart reversed polarizing ends;
I lead the wolves I was thrown to—
I tie my own hands;
The depth of the lesson lies not in how far you go,
But in how much you withstand.

Seasons

It was not I who truly walked away;
Strength from fire to remain,
Seasons fade, but I'm forever unchanged;
Hearts no longer chained, wings are free—
Like breezes on branches of trees,
Rising from darkness, to gather new roots from dust—
Dig deeper to see.

Take the Wheel

For the first time—
I just want to lean into the breeze,
Let it carry me,

Take me where it will;
Let someone else take the wheel—
Just for a little while.

Ashes of Grace

Ghost in the machine,
Haunting my own dreams,
Could die any moment—
The now is resolute, absolute,
No space to ponder whys or hows—
Only NOW,
Puzzle pieces float slowly, softly, numbly—
Snap suddenly into place,
Fall like ashes—
Into grace.

Embers

Inverted paper, blank on words,
Themes for rivers, twisting doors—
Handles, flow like feeling;
Flames' fuel, air for embers;
Darkness catapults hearts' remembrance...

Burn

I left no path untrodden,
I left no stone unturned;
Leading every dead end to the same place,
There was nothing left to do but burn.

How could I have seen ahead?
Eyes blinded by the sun.
A summer god I was,
Moving behind the barrel of a gun.

I cut my wings to spite the sun,
And silly as it sounds—
Even from ashes, I regret nothing—
It was too beautiful, too powerful,

It was everything that led me to come undone.

I Just Want To Live

I just want to live,
Only for the day, the moment;
Sun on my skin, bit of rain thrown in,
Zero consideration given—
To failing hearts, and who might go when;
I want that light to burn me from inside out,
If there was ever any doubt—
Of sincerity—
Surely it will melt away, merciful flames;
I end to begin, again and again—
There's still a level of now I've yet to swim in,

If I can't feel that edge, ever-present,
I just don't want anything;
I just want to live, right here,
In the now that's all there is;

Never

I stay, until the last remaining light;
Surrendered the ghosts,
But I'll never surrender the fight,
Just too much light to shine;
If that dawn shall take me, before a new world can arise,
It will find me on my own two feet, I'll never close my eyes.

Triggered

Trigger warnings—
Signs for the blind,
You're just running away—
From what's inside,
And calling it healing,
Just rerouting pain,
You'll never transcend yourself—
If you can't learn to dance in the rain.

-*Written with LOVE.*

Crests

Foaming wave crests,
Frozen like icicle dust;
The flag bearer cracks—
Emitting breath puffs,
We stand against the wind—
A long night creeps in.

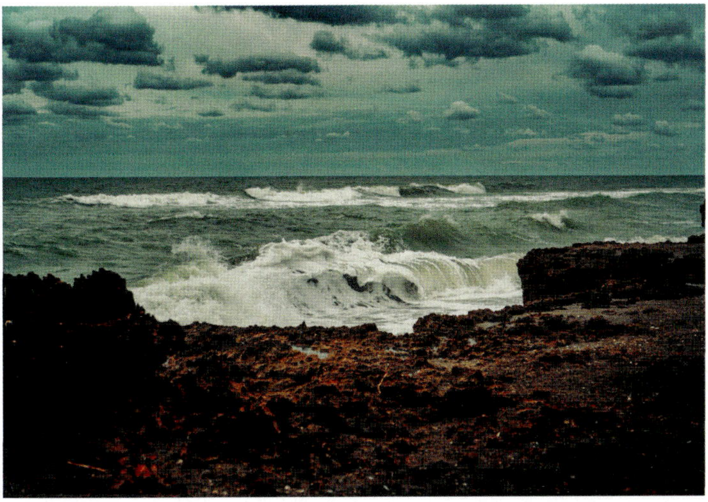

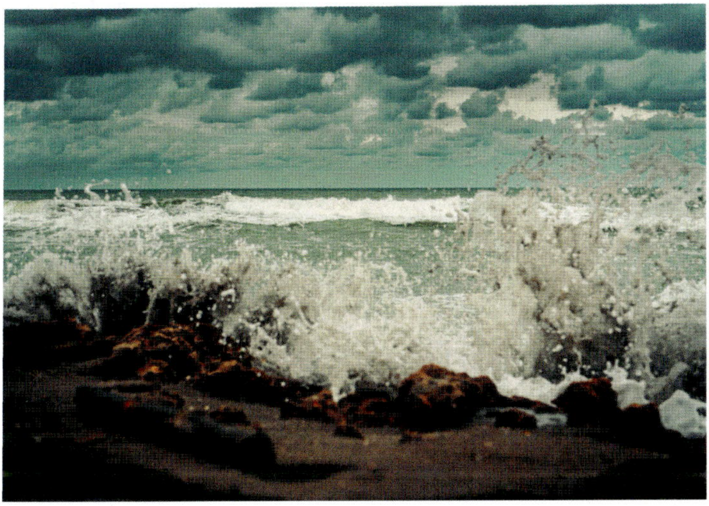

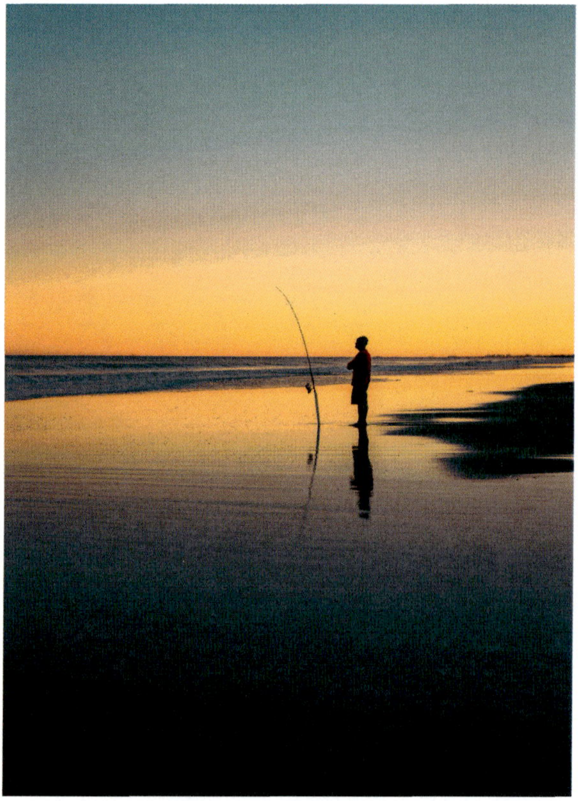

Winter

The blackest void nearly consumed the traveler, body and soul.

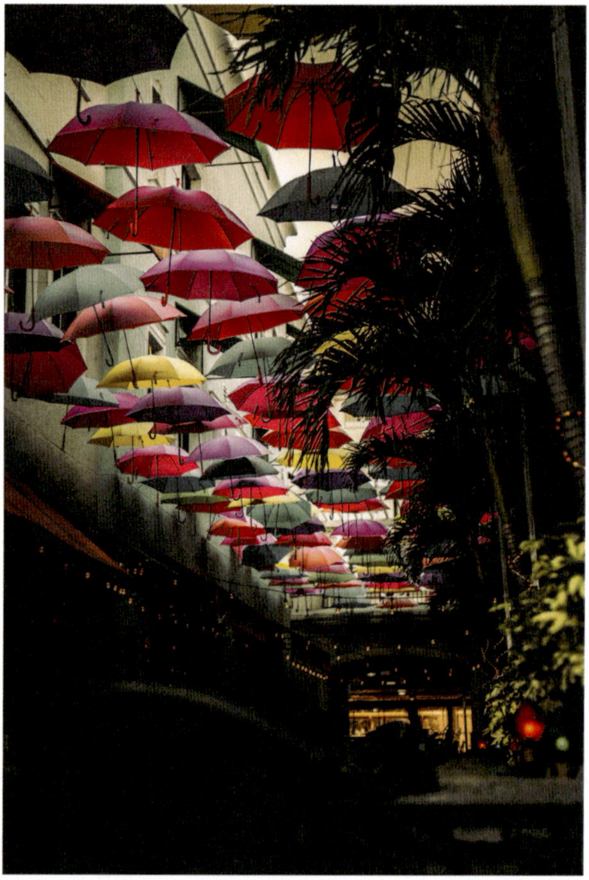

Umbrellas

Waiting—in the wings,
To sound alarms on unthinkable things,
Hidden—under colourful umbrellas,
Muted to the drab and weary that surround us,
Even the brightest umbrellas and coverings—
Can't hold the storm indefinitely;
Juggernaut of emotion,
How did motion become so static—
Living only in moments chosen by umbrella safety—
This can't be real, yet somehow it is;
I urge you, my friend, ditch those coverings—
Umbrellas can't withstand the wind—
But even hurricanes eventually end,
Better to dance, unapologetically, in the rain—
Than on the inside, rerouting unavoidable pain.

The Battle

I know this ocean, this blackest night—
All too well—
It seems brain chemicals can't resist picking another fight;
Drifting to sink, sinking to rise—
If I'm to continue to open my eyes,
Then what gives?
Who ever knows which roads will end up as dead ends?
Those overlords got nothing on this—
I've been going rounds with these shapes since 1986!
Maybe I should try screaming about it—
Seems to be working so well for the Earthings, doesn't it?!
There it is, my answer—
Silence, it is—
Ripples never stop if drops keep coming;
I know all too well, this is MY now,
Only I can fix it and climb out,
Even this thirty-seven-year-old scar on my wrist had that figured out;
So, for now, I'll just say good night—
Perhaps tomorrow brings a new kind of feeling,
Doubtful, I know, but still;
To that darkness within, that isn't my own,
I've just got to say:
You're a demon, you were sent to feed off my soul,
I want you to know—
If you want to take me,
You've no idea of the fight you've signed up for,
Even if you win, it'll be I who's really taken you.

Evermore

In stillness, in silence—
I feel the broken webs mending themselves;
Merciful golden light—
Restores connections—
Ones no heart could here explore;
Some doors may never open,
But doors and walls aren't forevermore;

What Gives?

What even is this—
This darkness?
This thickening quicksand,
Sinking through mud filled with vines,
Too asphyxiating to withstand;
What gives?
Gives—to give me an upper hand?

Murder Of a Crow

Lurking on ledges,
Screaming at crows, sitting on edges,
The thirteenth floor is the boundary's walled door—
Vocal cords fall silent, no matter how loud inside is.

Not a single crow took to air,
They stayed seated—
Left him there, and just stared;
Their silence engulfed his pain,
Melting away—
Sweet kiss of photons in dark, to dis-ignite the spark.

Eye of the Storm

Chaos all around,
Storm clouds closing in,
Lightning and flash floods,
Such dangerous wind;
Dropped pin on the map—
A place that doesn't even exist,
But still, there we were—
Somehow—
Safe in our cloud,
A storm's eye we somehow came upon;
Did we slip through space and time?
Who knows, what does it matter;
Just coming back down,
It didn't make sense—
Seeing floods and tree branches lying there,
When we hadn't even rain nor wind;
A safe haven we found,
And perhaps the secret wasn't a place,
But in our paired energy—
The Phoenix and the Wise Woods Witch,
We created a storm's eye, like alchemy.

Flow State

Picking locks in my mind,
Opening doors, forcing out ghosts—
Once bolted from within, now blown open,
Reaching up and in,
Nothing will keep these truths confined;
Restoring eyesight to my blind self,
Escaping the confines of lines,
My mind will flow like vines—
Flow state, transmute words from light.

Whiplash

Interdimensional whiplash, tension,
Free falling through space and time,
Continuum of endless searching within;
I can't say what you were thinking,
Leaving me these torches when my battery's dead—
What happened to me in that blackness?
I thought I'd wake up dead,
But my heart beats, and even now—
Somehow—
I'm beginning to thrive,
By some wonder, I'm still here, I'm alive.

Tamed Heart

I end—
Where I began,
Only refined—this time,
A tamed fire within my mind;
New beginnings are here—
Once more—
But I'll follow only the fire in my heart this time.

The Force of Flow

If I have to go—
I'd rather throw myself into the fray,
And not fade away,
There's still so much to do and say;
But if I am unable to crack this heart—
Ignite this spark—
Healing within,
Then I will NOT go quietly,
If hell must take me,
Then I shall make myself king—
Un-inverting their curses,
Restoring sight to blind leaves,
Just let them breathe,
Let me break free,
If this body can't withstand the fire—
I've been thrown to,
Then let it be—
The most absolutely, GLORIOUS fire to ever be!
Fireworks and implosions,
A new nuclear explosion,

A micronova!
Coming ascension,
If my heart isn't mended, in time—
Then let it burn, let it count for something more,
Let my fire light the way for even more—
More souls than we can dream of—
To come along—
It won't be long, now;
If I can't last the rest of this night—
Then let me burn as a new sun,
Let this collective break free, to WIN this fight;
I surrender, I let go, we can't have captains—
In this new world, only flow—
Which is never forced, this I know—
The Divine within tells me so,
Flow is never forced, but there's force to flow;[11]
If surrender is salvation, let it be, let me go.

---

1   [1] Inspired by the words and teaching of Carmela Marbella Roeschlein

Grammie

If I'd have known that fleeting view—
Into that hospital room—
Would be the last I'd ever have,
I'd have held onto those chairs to stay—
With everything I had.
Just turned seven years old,
So much light and love—I was the sun,
How little I knew, that how very soon—
My Divine Kingdom was about to crash into hell;
These hospitals—she was always in and out,
A bad heart, that's all such a young kid knew,
But this time had a different vibe—
Because I'd never seen Mommy cry like that.
I think that's what scared me,
Because I knew what was coming—
Like I needed to protect myself—in advance,
So I just crawled inside, my heart in a trance;
Early the next morning, a knock on my door,
I already knew it was Mommy and what she was there for;
The words left her mouth, my whole heart inverted—
My breath was gone—I couldn't utter a word;
My heart felt shattered, pieces so small—
And this was only the beginning of a decades-long fall.
'The Funeral'—a facade for the living,
And this was my first—
Some believed me too young,
To understand what was happening,
But I understood—even then—maybe better than most,
This grief would never leave,

It would become something to bear—
Many aren't able to transmute pain into power;
In I was led, so many flowers—
And there she was, looking NOTHING like herself,
Lifeless, of course, but this show just felt so wrong—
So cold and so formal, as if in a play—
And it wasn't rehearsal.
Why couldn't we just cry? Scream into the air?
"This sucks! She's gone!"
But no, let's play another song, as if that would fix it—
And that's when it sunk in—
The moment everything changed,
The moment from which my life was never the same.
And here I am, thirty-eight years later,
Crying for you, Grammie—
I wish you could see me.
So much has transpired,
I almost lost my life to a failing heart too,
But this is the thing, I've transcended myself,
I've retrieved my Divine Heaven—
By daring to walk through hells!
I was so young, but our connection was real,
So THANK YOU—
For being the start of the long road that led me back to myself;
I know I'll see you, on the other side—
One way or another—I love you—
It's been a wild ride, and I know you're watching with pride.

You can always find your way home...

The Rising

Surrender was salvation, and at long last,
the traveler found his way.

Frequencies

Boundaries set for self-preservation—
Are not an open invitation,
To call one out for not bearing their heart to the world;
There's no blind eye turned—
BELIEVE me, every inch of me burns,
When I hear of wars and hunger,
Children sobbing for their mother—
Who was taken away,
By men in planes,
Following orders of reptilian lords—
Cleverly disguised as leaders, guardians who care—
Just look into their eyes, there's just nothing there;
And yes, that's a terrifying truth to face—
But I just can't embrace—
The notion that somehow, I'M the problem—
Because I won't vote for this or that—
I won't wear a red OR blue hat;
There's an agenda, like it or not,
These demons won't stop till they take EVERY-THING you've got—
And broken your soul;
To each their own,
But friend, I implore you—
Tune it out, turn it off,
This doesn't mean drowning your heart out,
Quite the contrary—
You can hang onto those fear frequencies,
Or you can embody the change you want to see.

Vessels

Drops fall as tears,
As vessels for beings falling to Earth—
Falling to break—
Inside a shell,
To return to the sky—
To the stars beyond.

Splash

Rising, from the fall,
Axis inverted,
Can't wait for this set—
To usher new earth in;
Currents bring waves,
Arising to crash,
Learn how to surf—
Take joy in the splash.

Florida

Once upon a nightmare dream—
A man and his mouse—took paradise,
And slowly turned it into hell.
'La Florida', a flowery passion,
Like so many a place,
Destroyed like a fashion.
This mouse man is loved—

Loved and praised—
For stealing this land of beauty,
In his own deceptive way.
I remember a time, not too long ago—
My own ears heard a tour guide brag with bravado—
Of mouse man's trickery—
Fake names and a secret runway!
It's still there today, though much covered up—
Not far from the graveyard, of dismantled rides—
From your memories of youth!
That's right—they toss them away,
Dumped—behind a kingdom—and left to decay!
Skeletons of attractions, fractions of hearts—
It was all a façade—
Because they JUST DON'T GIVE A FUCK!
And fifty years later, it's out of control—
Keeping up with the Joneses ain't just a third mortgage—
It takes selling your soul!
Do you understand?
This land, they destroy more and more,
To sell you a dream—
Which no one seems to realize,
Is just a clever disguise—a sorry EXCUSE—
FOR HOW THEY'RE FARMING YOU!
Like all of those few—
The ones with control—
And they're not gonna stop,
Until they've consumed you—HEART AND SOUL!
This place was utopia,
And they tore it all down,
Then so many more clowns,
They came into town—to milk what was left;

There just isn't breath—or room to take it,
With so much space closing in,
Around MY OWN VERY HOME!
Just so some zombies can escape for a while—
To a fabricated retreat—
So billionaires feast on YOUR salaries,
Do you really think five figures is worth THIS misery?
They take all the trees,
We can't even breathe,
It's hotter and hotter without any breeze,
Let's wait for some water for over two hours—
Let's take five plus, for a three-minute ride!
This is your playground? Really—these RIDES?
Who ever taught you that playgrounds—
Were for waiting around, melting, all day—
For a three-minute round?!
Everywhere has been turned into everywhere else,
This heaven is now a concrete hell;
And I feel for you—honestly I do—
Because they've got hooks so deep,
There's very few who can refuse;
They even teach it, like specialty,
In their own precious school,
Which by some irony, it's right there—
Across from that graveyard of memories,
That so many shared;
And there's no one to blame, but those greedy lords,
Do you have any idea of the ride you're REALLY being taken for?
Once upon a nightmare dream,
A man and his mouse, took this paradise—
And slowly turned it into hell.

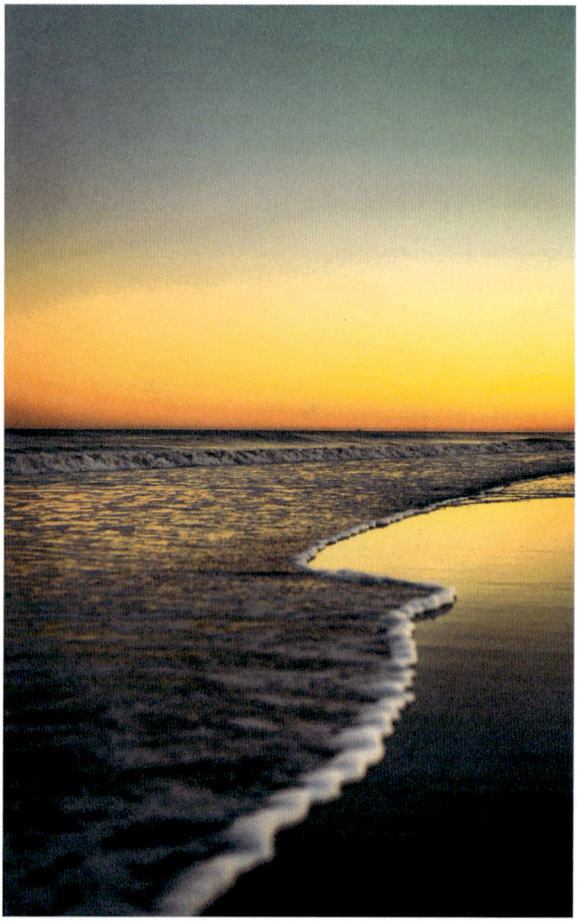

Bang the Drums
Co-written with Evelyn Lowell Prieto

My inner world reflected the outer—
Its current turbulence, just so much chaos—
Like trying to split atoms within—
Just to continue to exist;
I must confess—
My internal alchemy, had been—
More than just a little off kilter,
So much I had to just get off my chest,
Inverted again, collapsing into—
Internal darkness, once again,
Only this time I dared—
To feel it ALL—
To let that infinite darkness—
Stare straight into my soul,
And now I know—
There's nothing I can't bear,
So I've laid my spirit bare;
I'll go gentle on that darkness—
For it was I—
That darkness just couldn't withstand;
So let us go on, further into the NOW,
Let's drop these shackles and climb on out,
We are few, but soon to be many,
The bad-ass GODS of our own sovereignty!
Sun warm and golden,
Paddling out into oceans;
Let's conduct our own symphonies,
Bang the drum to only the rhythm of our heart-
beats.

Every One Hundred Years

Red birds, blue birds—
Lost in their own songs,
Beaks wide open—
Consuming droplets from the same pond,
Not realizing—ALL of them were conned;
Dark forces, clipping wings—
Of ALL these beautiful birds—
Injecting them with mind coverings;
The wings have left their solace,
Abandoned trees for cage,
Even sweetest birds have lost their way—
And mere suggestion they were fooled,
Causes them to rage;
"It's safety" they will say,
"Science" tells us so,
Sadly, "science" is only the facts—
Those forces want you to know;
Big brother always watching,
Discredit those who try to shed light—
Even tragic "accidents", are the plight of some;
Maybe you, the reader, are even triggered now,
Perhaps you want to write me off,
As someone spewing garbage,
I understand—these truths are horrifying—
But YOUR willful ignorance won't stop this from happening;
If you don't want to hear me,
Just listen to your soul—it already knows—
There's nothing that adds up about this at all,
And deep inside you know it—
They're zookeepers, we're just players in their show;
But it's not too late—to face these truths—

Reclaim your sovereignty, after all, you are DI-
VINE—
I PROMISE you—this all has another side;
Keep heart, my friends—
In the end, there's only love—
The rest, it falls away,
Endings are *always* painful—
That's how we get to the *beginning*.

The War Is Over

Was the war REALLY over? Could it REALLY be true this time? He was not accustomed to stillness—his whole life had been filled with turbulence.

He slowly meandered up a long hall, filled with doors to his left and right. Each doorway gave way to a view of a different memory.

One was filled with scenes of a heaven he knew so, so long ago. His dad lifting him high. His mom smiling, watching him build sandcastles. Kelly's on Revere Beach, Mom and Grammie in the front seat. He was loved—he *was* love.

Behind another door was scenes of loss. Pain. Innumerable bullies, and not just at school.

Doors to rage. Pain. More loss, upon loss, upon loss. More rage. Houses of mirrors—nobody could see him, to the point his own vision distorted.

He kept walking.

There were clouds and fog, and he came upon a great gap in the floor. He heard voices screaming at him, taunting him—"you'll never make the jump! There's less than a 1% chance!"

He was so exhausted. He'd fought so hard, there was nothing left, no energy with which to make this jump.

It took him a while, but as he'd known all along—he'd rather die trying. He'd rather fall into that abyss forever, than to waste away in fear. That 1% would drop to 0% if he didn't even try.

He leapt, with everything he had. He flew through time and space, in slow-motion. Everything went dark. But gradually, then suddenly, he could feel earth beneath his feet. He'd leapt through a door, and he was surrounded by the brightest sun imaginable. He'd eclipsed even himself.

He looked before him, and his eyes met his own. Eyes of the little boy, a sun of heaven, he'd thought he'd lost so long ago. He knelt and threw his arms around that boy.

"I've got you. You're safe. You made it. We made it."

They looked back across that gap, to everyone who lay behind them.

Yes. The war was, in fact, over. That would take some time to set in—to adjust, to accept it—but everything was okay now.

He took the little boy's hand.

"They didn't know what they did. They didn't understand. We need to forgive them now."

The little boy eagerly nodded.

"Let's light the way for them."

They held hands, as they walked into the unknown. NOTHING could touch them now. That boy had become an invincible man, and he would stop at nothing to light up the world.

Transcendence

Max stared down the long hallway. His first thoughts were of curiosity, as well as an inexplicable longing. This was immediately followed by fear of course, but he knew better than to listen to his previous conditionings, trying desperately to contain him.

Light was coming from the other end of the hall, and for a brief second, Max caught a glimpse of a glowing spiral. The bluish-hued shape seemed to vanish, as he began to walk toward where it had hovered.

The hallway was lined with floor-to-ceiling glass. Behind each glass panel, lights flickered.

A humanoid-shaped shadow behind the glass caused Max to stop abruptly. Moving closer to the window, he saw two men fighting in a crowded street.

Through the next window, there was a woman in the distance. She was standing near the edge of a great cliff. Realizing what she was about to do, Max began furiously banging on the glass.

A monotone voice spoke.

"You cannot help them. You must first help yourself."

Spinning around and around, Max sought the source of the voice. He found nothing. It spoke again.

"Something has brought you here. Continue."

"I can't just let her jump!"

"Look closer."

Pressing his face right to the glass, Max looked around the entire scene. The woman near the cliff had vanished, and the entire surroundings were changing before his eyes. A thick forest of trees appeared, and the same woman ran by, smiling, before disappearing around a corner.

"Closer," said the voice.

Scanning every corner of what was behind the window, Max noticed something he had looked right past before. A woman lay on the floor beneath the forest.

"It is merely a projection, you see. You were once as she is now. That is her journey. This is yours. Now come."

Further up the hall he went, looking at the scenes behind the glass. There were children tossing a ball. Tigers running through snow. A woman staring at the moon smiling, whilst across the hall from her, a man staring up at the moon longingly.

The rest of the hallway suddenly melted away. A large room was slowly replacing it, painting itself into existence before Max's eyes. A figure approached. They looked not unlike how humans seem to believe aliens should look.

"Follow me, you must see this."

The voice—the same as the one in the hallway—was coming from the being now standing before Max. They hadn't moved their mouth. Did they even have a mouth?

"I am just here for you. Stop questioning, only listen. Listen, and you will learn. Now follow, please."

Max followed. They passed basin after basin filled with coloured, glowing liquid. Other beings were around, some of them stirring the liquid.

Stopping in front of a large, gold basin, the being turned to Max.
"You must see this. You will learn whatever you are meant to know."

"Where is this place?"

"This is not a place. This simply *is*."

"What's your name?"

"Names are not a necessary evil here. Now look."

Max stepped forward and gazed into the basin. The liquid began to quickly swirl. The iridescent fluid began to float into the air, taking the shape of a tiny, corkscrew-shaped mini-galaxy. It was breathtakingly beautiful.

"This spiral is your tribe. The top of the spiral represents what you perceive as the future. The bottom, the past. When all the members of your tribe reach the top, you may ascend together."

"Ascend to what, exactly?"

"You already know the answer to that. You were created with that answer in your soul. When you are ready, step forward into the spiral."

Max only needed a moment to collect himself before stepping forward. The spiral began to spin around him. He raised his hand to touch it, but discovered it was intangible. The fluid slowly entered his hand, like a river that suddenly began to flow backwards. Turning and twisting, the spiral made its way entirely into Max's body. The spiral was in him, until he realized he *was* the spiral.
There were memories, some his own, and some which belonged to people he recognized. Some were of things that had not yet come to pass. Or *had* they?

Then Max understood. There were timelines that went in different directions for different individuals. His past might be someone else's future, and vice versa. The timelines themselves—their speed, direction, their infinite trajectories—were not what was important. All that mattered was the intersecting alignments between them, no matter how long or short. When enough of the collective elevated their spirals, they could ascend together.

Max awoke on the beach to the sound of dolphins playing nearby. He no longer needed to wait for anyone; they were the ones waiting—waiting for him to catch up. The spiraling stardust flowing through his veins brought him peace, at long last.

"Once More, With Feeling..."
Journal Entry | 2 - 4 April, 2024

Today is day six since the heart attack, as well as day six since I once again began down the long, gruesome path to full sobriety. I've not slept more than an hour here and there, and have been unable to get any food down. My body is breaking down in every possible way, and my spirit is cracking. Quitting is not my style, but I see zero way forward.

I summon the strength to pull down an old blanket from my closet. My great-grandmother, Lillie, hand-made it for my grandfather about one hundred years ago. My grandfather and father subsequently passed on with it covering them. I was attempting to go in another direction.

I pull it over myself. There are not words for how incredibly weak and helpless I feel. I begin speaking aloud to my angels: my dad, my aunt, my cat Blue. My grammie, who passed when I was seven. My maternal grandfather whom I never met. My great-grandmother who had made the blanket. I called on everyone I'd lost, and every connection I have here and now.

"Please, I can't die yet. Wrap your arms around me."

I allow myself to begin slipping into sleep. If I was going to meet death, I refused to meet him with fear—I'd be staring him right in the face.

I woke less than two hours later. The sun was coming up. Why can't I just sleep? This is *maddening*, and I am *breaking*. I can't handle this. I reach for a pen and notebook. Let's try for some release, I figure.

~

TUESDAY

I'm not off the rails, I'm not even in the train. There seems to be no limit to what my body can withstand. WHY? But my mind, it's cracking, and my heart is shattered in every possible way.

I'm alone. The void within quickens; I feel like it's consuming me. I'm pretty sure it is. I need to find a way through, but I can't see anything but blackness. How can I climb up again? I can't keep experiencing these indescribable glimmers of heaven, just to crash back to hell.

I know anything is possible, but is there enough will to continue? I feel like I've got nothing left. From where can I possibly draw energy? My breath—my life force—is so limited.

I don't feel anger this time. I feel lost. Indifferent. Am I hopeless?

I scare myself. I know what I'm capable of. I'm a killer. I've lied. I've manipulated. I've stolen. I've hurt almost everyone I love. I am a lifelong addict and substance abuser.

I've painted myself into corners so tightly, there's barely room to breathe. I think right now all I can do is wait for the paint to dry.

Despite it all, I know in my soul that I never entered into any of it with intent to harm. I know in the greater picture that part doesn't matter much, but it does bring me solace to know.

When I can center all of it, I feel my authentic self shining through my whole being, and I feel light. I observe how others respond to me, and I can't even believe it sometimes, that someone like me could have that potential impact.

It feels like lightning, and it courses through me, and electrifies my soul. When I know I've brought someone even a moment's peace, I feel purpose, and it lights me up. It gives me this indescribable boost to create even more.

I used to want to save the world. Destroy the matrix. Bring death to falseness. But I know now, I can only save myself. Nobody needs to destroy the false matrix, that fucker will burn itself down. It's already dying.

There is no world to save, but everyone is a world unto themself. If I can save myself, I can be a light unto others, so they can save themselves. That is what ultimately saves me—my purpose.

I've made my bed and I've got to lie in it, but I can't let myself die in it. I can't. I have to fix this. I see no way, no way through. All I can do right now is hold on. I have to have faith I can fix my body. I don't even know how to have faith at the moment.

I'm terrified of crashing again. I cannot fall even one more time, because I won't get up. So, for now, I'm just going to hold on.

I could fix it; I know it's possible. I could walk right into heaven. I could light the world up. I could see everyone I love again. My body would match my soul, as I've always known.

Possible, no doubt. But, how? I need energy. I need resolve. I need clarity. There's no map, and I feel alone, but I know—I can't let the darkness take me.

~

WEDNESDAY

Still no sleep. I can't endure that much longer. My heart rate is okay at the moment, but my chest is so tight. My body is screaming. I feel so close to death and I've got to hold on.

What gives?

There's no anger anymore. It broke away. I

don't know where it went, but I guess it doesn't matter.

I'm weak. Just holding this pen is a feat. I'm so alone, and I just don't want to talk to anyone. Nobody understands, and I guess that's fine.

I want my dad. He would understand. I still get hit with waves of 'how is he just not here?'

When I was so young, he'd rub my legs when I got Charlie Horses in the middle of the night. I could always wake him for anything. He was so gentle, and nobody has ever been so patient with me, until now. He was the ocean that cooled my flames. Maybe I haven't really let him go. I can't keep doing this.

How many trees had to die so I could carpet a room with tissues? They're probably not even made from real trees anymore.

The trees don't cry out when someone carves silly hearts into their flesh. They simply endure. They don't ask for help; they wait for someone to ask "what's wrong?", and almost no one ever does.

Trees give and never ask for anything in return. They help each other without expectation or obligation. Maybe we could all learn from trees.

These roots grow deeper, but I can't withstand these flames much longer. Far beyond the pale of the center blue, and there will be no return.

I must learn to burn more completely, or I'll be lost.

I just can't care anymore. What else can crack? I don't fucking care at all. And yet, I would still die for anyone in a heartbeat. Can I die for myself? I really fucking tire of being a living, breathing contradiction.

I want to break the chains, but I'm too weak, and all I can do is lie here and keep breathing.

~

THURSDAY

Darkness, like never before. I see lightning behind my eyelids. Adrift on an ocean, such vastness. It's a fine dance of self-rescue and surrender.

I have this feeling in my solar plexus, this tugging, as if my insides are getting turned around. I am desperate for the sleep that never seems to come.

Time dilates into an infinite now, and I'm staring into sheer darkness—an unyielding terror. I remain calm, it feels too much for my heart. I am floating through space, alone. I can't long for anything, I can only feel one emotion: DEFIANCE. Defiance of all who would demand an explanation. I answer to NO ONE. I will burn this chess board down—for nobody but myself—and for my soul, there is no other way through.

Let's feel what it is to burn...

~

We wake as clay,
We rattle these cages hands could never break,
Most will never look past the bars.
There is ages before the coming dawn—
But I KNOW it will come,
We can't be afraid of coming undone.

~

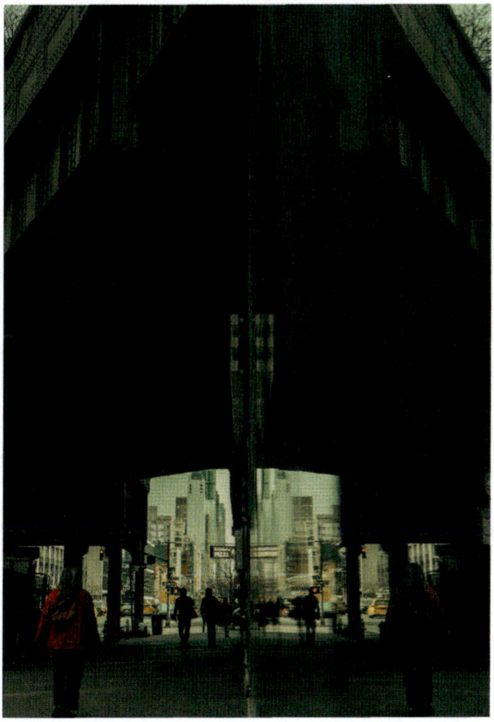

Extended Photo Section

Greater storms approach, attempting to blacken the coming dawn—but that dawn WILL arrive, it is simply unstoppable. Despair will call to you, but you must bend—never break.

For this next part, you're going to have to be very, very brave. Keep heart, my friends, always…

Come around, sundown–let's ride out this night—to reach a new dawn's light...

Be
the
light
you
needed

Portland
Head Light-
house on
Portra 160
film

The view is always relative.
Taken from High Line, Manhattan—March 2024

Distant shores beckon, crowded streets disperse; the observer left to the peace within misery, the pleasure within pain—the infinity of internal alchemy...

Dissolution into oneness...

Earth is the roots to which I return, when that intensity of my flames too brightly burns...

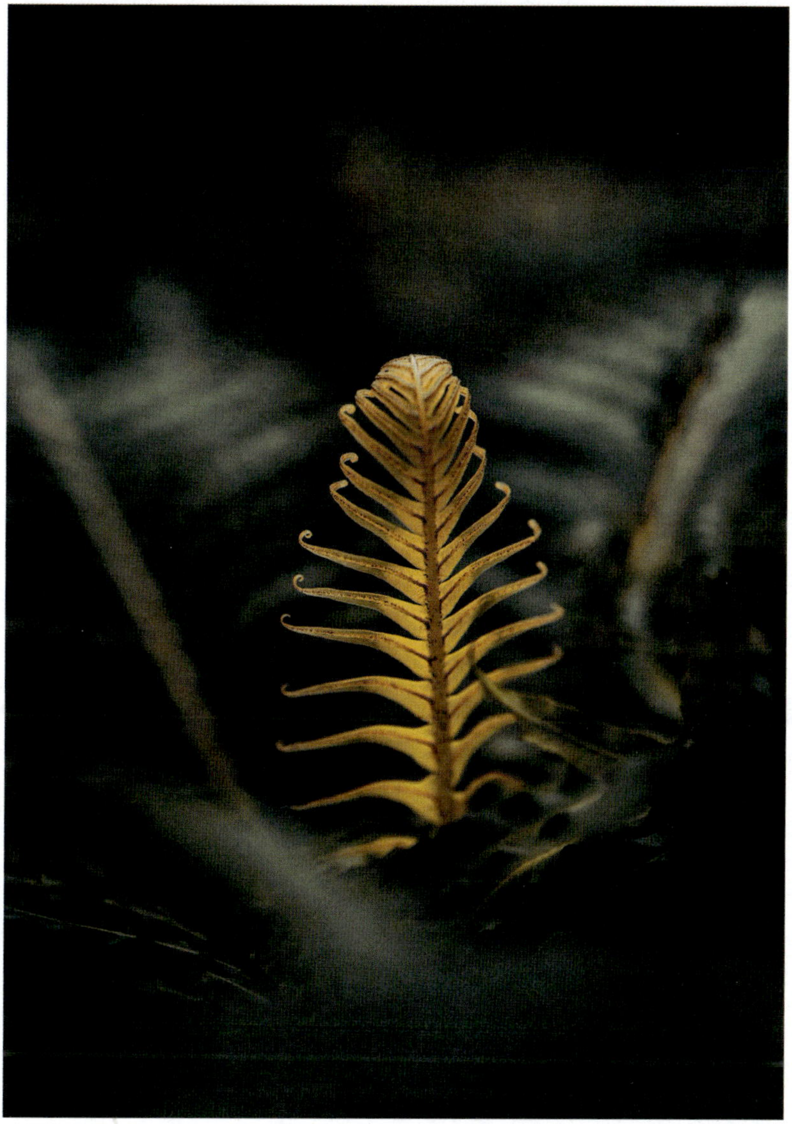

Purify as fire, as the sun;
Burn it up til nothing remains but One...

Turn to the earth to ground you,
Instead of the false machinery which surrounds you.

Important life hacks:

Light is not the cure for darkness; the cure can only be found within that darkness.

The remedy for grief is the grief itself.

Pain can convert to power, an invaluable source of fortitude and strength—a tenacity which can lead to salvation.

You are your own saving grace.

Photos snapped in New York City, March 2024

In the quiet noise, in the stillness of the void, keep it moving

*Snapped from
Cocoa Beach,
Florida*

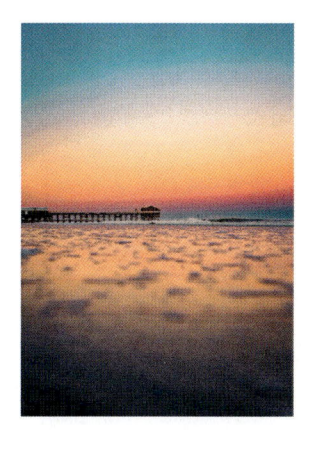

Taken from NYC Metro, March 2024

Why do we feel so alone in a crowd of faces; tame that chaos, embrace the peace within—begin again...

Taken from Pier 57, NYC, March 2024

We look in the same directions, but we see very different things...

Occulus, NYC. Taken July 2023

Florida gulf coast

The ones we love will always hurt us the most, and that goes both ways. Some may call this a darker side of love, but this is where the most profound lessons lie. Whatever pain may be, we can honour our own hearts by committing fully to those lessons.

Cocoa Beach, Florida

I knew fortitude as a refuge within, as something entirely different—long before the war began. When it ended, I had been washed clean, yet that fortress remained—unchanged by tide or season—for it was I who'd held those walls, all along.

The dawning of a new age is upon us…

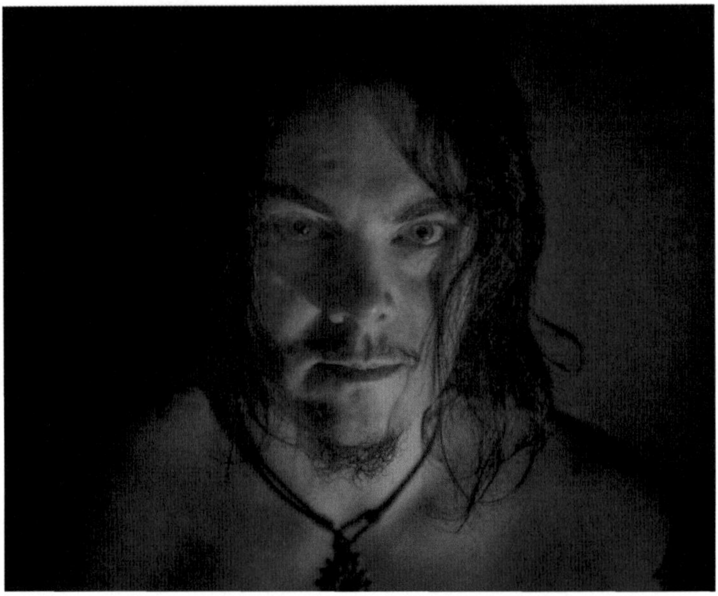

About the Author

Hi, I'm Tyler! I'm a full-time writer and visual artist originally from just north of Boston, currently residing in Florida.

Writing began for me at age seven, as a form of therapy for dealing with the loss of my grandmother. It went from a near-constant lifelong hobby to a profession several years ago, when I took up ghost writing, and also began writing under several pen names. My poetry compilation, "Parallel to Sundown" marked the first release in my own name. "Static Flow" is the follow-up.

Poetry is a constant for me, but I also write plenty of fiction. When not writing, you can usually find me with a camera in my hand, traveling as often as possible. My biggest loves are art and spending time with my family and close friends, including my cat—Catniss.

There are additional volumes of poetry in the works, along with an autobiography, as well as fictional novels—so stay tuned for more!

Also available:

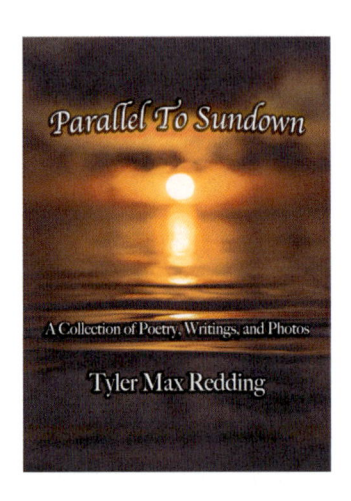

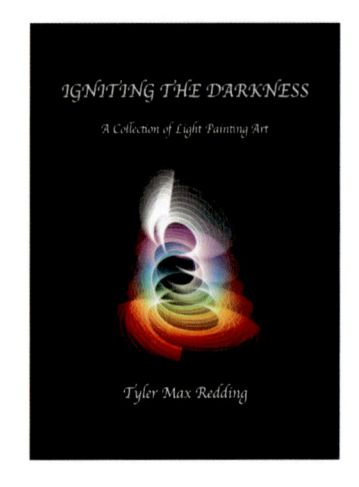

Parallel To Sundown
A Collection of Poetry, Writings, and Photos
Tyler Max Redding

IGNITING THE DARKNESS
A Collection of Light Painting Art
Tyler Max Redding

Let's connect!

linktree.com/tylerismaximus

Afterword—Selected Poems of My Father: James B. Rice

Introduction

My dad grew up in a small town in Downeast Maine. I have countless, prized memories of road trips up there from where I grew up, just north of Boston. The stories he and my grampie would tell—to my young mind—there was nothing more I wanted to hear.

I never got to meet my paternal grandmother, she passed on when I was still a baby. I wish very much I could have known her, if even for a short time. My dad gave me the next best thing—making sure I knew her through his memories.

One memory of her that he never shared, however, was the very last time he saw her alive. She spent the last months of her life in a diabetic coma, never awakening again. The last time my dad went to the hospital to see her, he sang to her, and as she lay there—unconscious—in the bed she would later pass away in, tears streamed down her face. My father broke down. He simply couldn't handle it; not many could in that situation.

I only heard of this from my mother, a few

years after my dad's passing. I'd never known

he'd carried this pain with him—a brand of pain I came to know all too well—as I sat by his side, reading to him, as he lay slowly dying.

One of the things that came into my possession upon my father's death was an almost empty, very old, hard-bound journal—with a handwritten note inside the cover:

"To Jim, when you write your poems—keep them in this. Love, Mom."

He never did get around to writing much in it, but I write in it on occasion—things I will always keep private. It's a small way of keeping my connection to the stories of memories of the sweet woman I never got to meet, alive; a way to honour my father by someday completing it.

My dad entered the Air Force one year after high school, and served eight and a half years. He very well may have been a lifer, had they not tried to station him in Alaska. It was just too far from family for him, so he requested—and was granted—an Honorable Discharge.

He settled in a suburb just north of Boston, and found himself in need of a career path, since the Air Force didn't work out as planned. He ended up working in finance in downtown Boston for close to forty years. Numbers came naturally to him. He always—however—kept up with writing his poetry, something he'd begun at a young age, just as I would go on to do. He had a flair for using the simplest words in eloquent ways, reminding the reader to not forget the beauty that constantly surrounds them.

To Dad: I could not have asked for a better father. You taught me patience, and from that patience came perseverance. You were gentle and kind, but FIERCELY protective when the moment called for it. Not that we never had our disagreements, but in the endless end, everything worked out just fine. Every promise made has been kept, and always will be. There will be no roads left untaken.
I see you in my eyes every time I glance my reflection. I feel your unique brand of humour within myself. Your empathy. Your intensity. Your unconditional love. I've inherited your incredible way to use words in the most powerful way—to heal. Thank you for everything.

On my honour, I will fulfill my purpose. Until we meet on the other side, I send my undying gratitude and love. *ALWAYS*.

-Tyler Max Redding Henson Rice

Poetry by James B. Rice

Friends

Two creatures lived together,
And they tried to keep each rule;
Quite often they succeeded,
The jackass and the mule.

The folks who lived around them,
Tried to tell them what to do;
It always is that way in life,
It's the same for me and you.

In sports they both competed,
Sometimes the mule would win;
Some thought that he was cheating,
And cheating is a sin.

So, as you read this sordid tale,
And wonder where to go;
Perhaps a little stay in jail,
Would be a way to know.

What's the point of this sad song?
How can you keep the rule?
Best admit you're a jackass,
Than to be a suffering mule.

A Lesson

I saw a swan swimming,
Alone at Flax Pond;
Why was he alone,
And then the light dawned.

A swan is a creature,
That mates once in life;
He doesn't change partners,
At the first sign of strife.

When his or her partner,
Gets ready to die;
The one who's remaining,
May give a short sigh.

The next time you notice,
One swan swimming by;
Maybe it's <u>you</u>,
Who'll give out a sigh.

There's no power in pining,
Or waiting to heal;
You may need to think,
Where is my next meal?

One thing that folks wonder,
Each and every day;
"If somebody hurts me,
Then who's gonna pay?"

Maybe the lesson, to be learned from the swan,

Is no matter what happens, we need to go on.
We go for a swim, or maybe a walk,
We find a friend, with whom we can talk.

Life wasn't meant, to be lived just for "me",
We need to go out and see what is to see.
There might be something, to provide us some cheer,
It may be at a distance, or perhaps very near.

If, when the day's over, you feel kind of sad,
Or maybe distressed, maybe you're even mad;
It's time to rethink, what should I do?
Perhaps I could bring a smile to you.

Now I often think of that swan all alone,
Did he sit and mope, like a dog with no bone;
No, the swan goes, once more to Flax Pond,
He doesn't wait to see who will respond.

Maybe, today, this verse is for you,
You may be thinking, what should I do?
Get yourself moving—do what you can,
For you this may be a far better plan.

Life

Just a few thoughts, as onward you go,
Of the last few weeks, and all of this snow;
How easy it is to get down on life,
All of its troubles and all of its strife.

Seems so much goes wrong—good turns to bad,
We're so quick to turn from happy to sad;
A thought occurred to me—a short time ago,
That maybe I'm missing a fact I should know.

The storms which have come are part of our being,
What is it here, that I am not seeing?
We've seen lots of snow, which has fallen down,
It's fallen all over every city and town.

Yet, every day, the blessings still fall,
God is still looking over us all;
He sends the sunshine, along with the snow,
We just need to listen for His voice, you know.

Maybe the answer is simply to pray,
Put yourself in His hands every day;
Why be discouraged, when He's given a way,
To be more content as we live every day.

Well Done

This is a story that you need to hear,
The whole tale I have learned;
It's somewhat exciting, a little bit wild,
The day the turnip burned.

The story took place in Monmouth, Maine,
Nobody was watching the pot;
First the pot boiled, then the pot burned,
Things were getting quite hot.

The poor little turnip began to turn black,
Even much blacker than ink;
As the smoke starts to clear,
All that you knew, was "it's starting to stink".

Now you've heard the story, beginning to end,
There is no more I can tell;
Just don't let your pot simmer too long,
Or it may blow all to _ _ _ _ .

Family

Sometimes, when life gets busy,
As we go upon our way;
We think of what's important,
As we decide to go or stay.

We think of all the memories,
That go back to years ago;
It was easy to be happy,
Whether things were fast or slow.

We think of little children,
These days, they all are grown;
They're part of all those memories,
As the years have quickly flown.

We remember weddings, funerals,
Birthday parties by the score;
We think of Christmas parties,
That don't seem to happen anymore.

Perhaps we should think back,
Turn the clock back if we can;
Get together and be happy,
That would be a better plan.

Time is quickly fleeting,
We must try as best we can;
To get it all together,
To act out a master plan.

It's so easy to get angry,
To say "I do not care";
Suddenly we look around,
And nobody else is there.

Life passes by so quickly,
Not really time to hold a grudge;
Sometimes it is so silly,
What we decide to judge.

The best thing any of us,
Could do to help ourselves;
Would be to let the bad things go,
And act like little elves.

You know the elves do work for Santa,
No time to cry or moan;
Before you even know it,
You'll be left all alone.

A Simple Lesson

Twas a hot afternoon in the month of July,
The year was twenty thirteen;
To a garden I came at the edge of the woods,
I'll try to tell what I'd seen.

To the garden there came a young, blond-haired girl,
She was only eleven years old;
From Oklahoma she came to this far away place,
And now the tale can be told.

In the garden that day this little blond girl,
Pulled up the grass and the weeds;
She tried to make it look better you see,
By doing a few, small good deeds.

The story I want to tell you about,
Is just an everyday tale;
Her name is Kenzie—you don't need to shout,
And you don't need to weep or to wail.

Perhaps if I'd been half asleep that day,
Or maybe paying no mind;
I might have missed the little good deeds,
From somebody just being kind.

As I stood there, watching her work,
She went and brought me a chair;
By this simple kind deed, it taught me at least,
It doesn't take much to care.

So Kenzie, I thank you today,
For doing what you thought best;

As you grow up, just stay as you are,
And you'll pass the most difficult test.

Sometimes in life we must be aware,
A lesson is there to be learned;
If we just help out wherever we can,
Someone's respect will be earned.

A Short Story

I'm here to tell a story,
That you have never heard;
There is no need to worry,
I won't make you learn a word.

One day, a few short months ago,
While walking down the street;
In the window of a beauty shop,
Was something really neat.

In that window was a hand-drawn scene,
That really made me smile;
So different from the common scenes,
I knew twas by a child.

For several weeks as I passed by,
This window once again;
This picture brightened up my day,
Like a visit with a friend.

One day as I went on my way,
A lady stood outside the shop;

I asked if she knew who drew the scene,
That nothing else could top.

I learned that the artist,
Was just a little girl;
She loved to draw, to create scenes,
Which brightened up the world.

As time passed by,
One day I saw, the picture was not there;
It was like a cloudy, rainy day,
When no one seemed to care.

Just a day or two ago,
I did learn at last;
The name of her who drew so well,
That picture from the past.

Her name is Jaylyn,
All of you may hear of her some way;
Perhaps she'll brighten up your world,
As she did mine that day.

Felix

He was only a gecko,
But he was my friend;
His silence was golden,
From beginning to end.

When life got exciting,
Commotion throughout;

Felix was quiet,
As he ran about.

For him, life was simple,
Just eat, sleep, and run;
Each day like another,
And then life was done.

On the fifth of February,
In Two thousand six;
His short life was over,
No more of his tricks.

He'd sit in my hand,
And run up my arm;
With never a cross word,
Nor caused any harm.

So, Felix, I miss you,
Guess I always will;
During great commotion,
I'll think of you still.

Apple Juice

There is a story about a girl,
The story needs to be told;
She loved to drink apple juice,
All that she could hold.

She grew up to be an apple tree,
She blossomed in the spring;
Apples grew on every branch,
And made her want to sing.

She said "why would I be a tree,
I'd rather be a girl;
So I could jump both up and down,
And do a little twirl".

She kept on drinking apple juice,
While moving on through life;
She grew up to be a moose,
With all that crazy strife.

"I don't want to be a moose", she said,
"I'd rather be a girl;
Who likes to drink her apple juice,
Than to be a thirsty girl.

What is a Friend?

The thought had been a-hovering,
Just outside my head;
"Who have been my truest friends,
Among the living and the dead?"

What has made the difference,
As I look back o'er the years;
It's those who've been constant,

Through the laughter and the tears.

Anybody can pretend,
To be something they're not;
Because it's just themselves they fool,
They're easy marks to spot.

To have a friend that you can trust,
You, too, must be a friend;
There is no need to question fact,
From beginning to the end.

Perhaps the best thing one might do,
Would be to <u>be</u> a friend;
Because, to do otherwise,
A wrong message you do send.

When you see a person who,
Is doing what they can;
To help themselves and other folks,
That's part of God's great plan.

It's quite easy to complain,
While sitting, doing naught;
That's sometimes how we lose a friend,
Without giving it a thought.

When we're so busy judging others,
There's no room to forgive;
That is how a friendship dies,
Much more "take" than there is "give".

At last the time has come for me,
To let this message end;

I'd like to hope, once reading this,
You'll still count me as a friend.

The White Dove

Once, while working in the churchyard,
In the year two thousand five;
Twas a beautiful fall morning,
The kind you're glad that you're alive.

There was flying near a window,
Alone, a pure white dove;
I watched it as it flew by,
In the blue sky up above.

It flew up near a window,
Of course it couldn't go inside;
It approached another window,
I watched it as it tried.

The dove continued flying,
To windows three and four;
And I began to wonder,
At its actions more and more.

I then approached the Pastor,
And told him of the bird;

I asked him for a meaning,
Or was this all absurd.

He told me that the white dove,
Which was flying still;
Might mean the Holy Spirit,
Trying to do the Father's will.

I asked him what he meant by that,
As I tried to understand;
I recall his answer still,
As before you now I stand.

"Perhaps God is telling us,
Not to shut His Spirit out;
To be alert to God's messages,
As we travel all about."

Now that many months have passed,
I still recall that dove;
Just maybe he was telling us,
Of our Father's lasting love.

As we exist upon this earth,
The years are passing fast;
We need to pay attention,
To the things that really last.

Maybe God could use you,
If you'd listen to His voice;
Perhaps signs are all around you,
You just need to make a choice.

Today might hold the moment,
When God will show a sign;

Just to make you pay attention,
You know God is Divine.

He knows your every feeling,
He knows what you've gone through;
He will guide you in life's pathway,
If <u>His</u> choice is what you <u>do</u>.

–I wish to acknowledge Pastor D. Kevin Adams, who on this occasion, helped me to see beyond what my eyes alone were seeing. -James B. Rice 3/9/2006

A Picture From a Memory

Twas early and the rising sun,
Showed through the stillness of the morn;
The cloudless sky was brightest blue,
As the sun rose to meet the dawn.

The stand of birches, pure and white,
Seemed to enhance the sky so blue;
As I gazed out on the fading night,
I wasn't sure what I should do.

Somehow the picture wasn't done,
Quite like an unfinished symphony;

Or perhaps a painting, incomplete,
Twas all a mystery to me.

And then, from out the morning sky,
A beautiful, red cardinal flew;
And landed in the birches nigh,
Began to do what cardinals do.

His song resounded through the earth,
The light of day began to arrive;
The red cardinal, the white birches,
The blue sky too—God is alive!

–Written from a memory of my stay in a hospital bed in 2003. Awakening at 5:00 am, I glanced out my window and this, this poem was born. -James B. Rice 3/24/2006

James B. Rice

~ 10 November, 1937 – 25 June, 2019 ~

No roads left untaken. *Always*.

Dedications

Henson Family—In Loving Memory Of:

Laura (Hodge) Ingram & Arthur Ingram

Alice "Nama" (Darrell) Henson & Geoffrey S. Henson

Doris Mae (Ingram) Henson & Arthur Melvin Henson

Baby Arthur Henson
Dawn E. (Henson) Esrkine
William "Billy" Walker
Carol A. (Walker) April & Peter April
James "Jim/Jimmie" B. Rice
Anne Shirley "Moppet" (Henson) Lowell &
    Robert "Bob" Ferguson
Barbara (Walker) Granese
David "Davy" Dickerson
Dennis A. Trenholm
Thomas "Tommy/Tom" Dunlop

As well as all ancestors who came before them.

Rest in paradise, until we all meet again.

Henson Family—In Loving Honour Of:

Sandra Darlene (Henson) Rice
Rolane Henson
Candice "Candy" (Henson) Dunlop
Cheryl (Henson) Bloch & Tom Bloch
  Miranda (Bloch) Terry & Eric Terry & Family
  Justin Bloch & Family
  Adam Bloch
Darrell Henson & Karen Campbell
  Darrell Henson & Family
    Ryan Henson
  Kristen Henson & Family
  Joel Campbell & Family
  Thomas Casey & Family
Laura Jean (Henson) Dickerson
  Susan Dickerson Lyons & Billy Werth & Family
    David Lyons & Luz Dubuc Lyons & Family
    Michael Lyons & Stephania Lyons & Family
    Richard Lyons & Alycea Landry & Family
  Sean McCabe & Family
Judith "Judy" (Henson) Moody &
    Robert "Bobby" Moody
  Kevin Moody & Kim Moody
    Steven Moody & Family
    Jennifer Moody
  Amy Beth (Moody) Palhares &
    Manuel "Manny" Palhares
  Jacob Palhares
  Nathan Palhares
Gail (Henson) Trenholm
  Nicole Trenholm & Family
    Allison Schofield & Family

Charlotte Trenholm
　　　Connor Trenholm
David Henson & Robin Henson
　　Eric Henson & Family
　　Dana Henson & Family
　　Shannon (Henson) Quinn &
　　　　Patrick Quinn & Family
　　　Evelyn Zungy
　　　Lydia Zungy Quinn
Harry Esrkine & Family
　　Patricia "Patty" (Esrkine) Drillis & Family
　　　Matthew "Matt" Drillis & Family
　　Marc & Kim Erskine
　　　Elizabeth Erskine
Carol Shaw
　　William "Willy Bill" Walker & Family
　　Debbie Walker & Family
　　Paul Walker & Family
Trudy & Family
　　Charlie & Family
Lori Landry
　　William "BJ" Landry & Family
　　Anthony Landry
James "Jimmy" Granese
　　Daniel Granese & Family
　　　Chad Granese
　　　Danielle "Dani" Granese
　　Sue Granese
　　　Charlie Creighton & Family
　　Linda (Granese) Austin & Sean Austin
　　　Laura Mae (Austin) Oliver & Rick Oliver
　　Kathy (Granese) Moriarty & Brian Moriarty
　　　Michael Moriarty

Robin Lemieux & Family
James "Jimmy" Lowell & Susan "Sue" Lowell
  Michelle Lowell & Family
Evelyn Lowell Prieto & Family
  Roman Prieto
  Lucia Prieto

Also, in honour of all minor children whose names will not be placed into print at this time, and all other living descendants.

Rice Family—In Loving Memory Of:

Ezra K. Rice & Lillie M. (Batron) Rice

George W. Stolte & Elizabeth E. (Prizeman) Stolte

Carl Vincent Rice & Gertrude Adelaide (Stolte) Rice

George V. Rice
  Cherry Gay Rice
  Theresa Lynn Rice
James "Jim/Jimmie" B. Rice
William "Billy" H. Rice
William "Billy" Edwards
Theodore W. Johnson

Marian V. (Rice) Bartlett & Harlan A. Bartlett
Celia Fern Rice
Samuel Ezra Rice

Elizabeth F. Stolte
George W. Stolte
Charles H. Stolte

As well as all ancestors who came before them.

Rest in paradise, until we all meet again.

Rice Family—In Loving Honour Of:

Sandra Darlene (Henson) Rice
Carol (Rice) Johnson
  Norman Edwards & Family
    Amber Edwards & Family
    Khayla Edwards & Family
    Emma Edwards & Family
    Erin Edwards & Family
  Pearl Thomas & Family
  Christina Edwards Gurney & Marc Gurney
    Kyle Gurney
    Nicholas Gurney
  Catherine Johnson & Partner Daniel

The living descendants of George V. Rice and
    William H. Rice

Also, in honour of all minor children whose names will not be placed into print at this time, and all other living descendants.

Redding Family—In Loving Honour Of:

Lacie "Lj/Jessie" Redding
Catniss Everyjay

Redding Family—In Loving Memory Of:

Blue
Isis
Stitch
Shadowboxer
Ghost
Samantha "Sam"
Smokey
Snowball
Dallas "Cowboy" B.
Felix
Tequila
Maxwell
Gex
Hurley & All Tankmates
Many Goldfish & Bettas
Sarkomand & Tree Frog Friends
Thumper
Mr. Peepers

Rest in paradise, until we all meet again.

To my eleventh great-grandfather—Stephen Hopkins:

You survived a shipwreck due to a hurricane. You incited an uprising on the island you took refuge on and somehow talked your way out of being executed.

Shakespeare made a mockery of you in "The Tempest".

You returned to England to discover your wife had died.

You still, however, had the courage to set sail on the Mayflower, in search of a better life, free from persecution for your beliefs. I admire that.

I do not, in any way, condone the actions of stealing the land of The Native Peoples who were already here, or what was done to them—I DESPISE it. However, everyone has only ever done the best they could at the time, a truth that is difficult for many to accept.

So, thank you—to you—and every other ancestor, for having the strength to persevere—so I could be right here, right now—fulfilling my own purpose, right on time; purpose to myself, to the collective, and to my own bloodlines. I send my eternal love and gratitude to all, through space and time—in all directions.

The ones we love remain with us, for love itself lives on. Our very cells possess the essence of our ancestors; they are never far.

In memory of all those who persevered, so we all could be here; In honour of all those living, and of all those to come.

Special Thanks To:

Lacia "Lj"
Mom
Catniss
Auntie Ro
Carmela
Charlotte
Evelyn
Katie "KT Bee"
Berol
Dr M.

Above all, my angels.

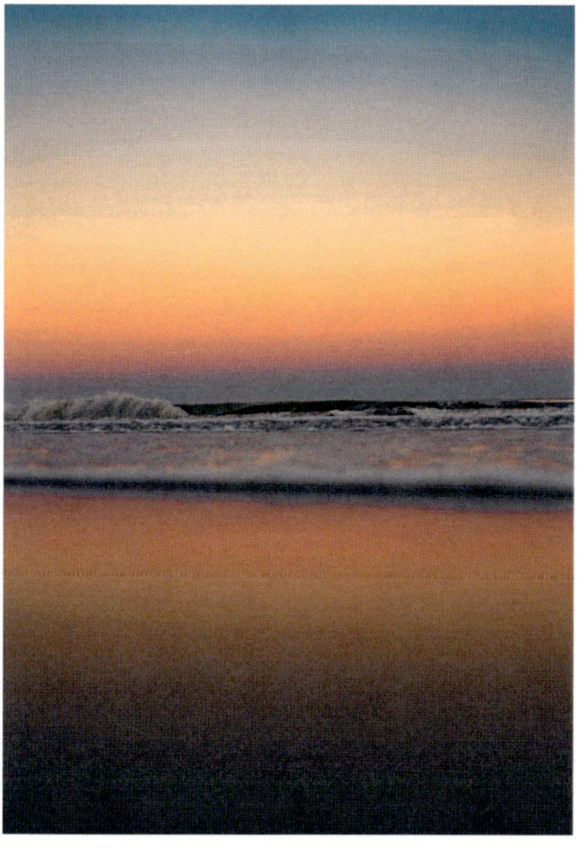

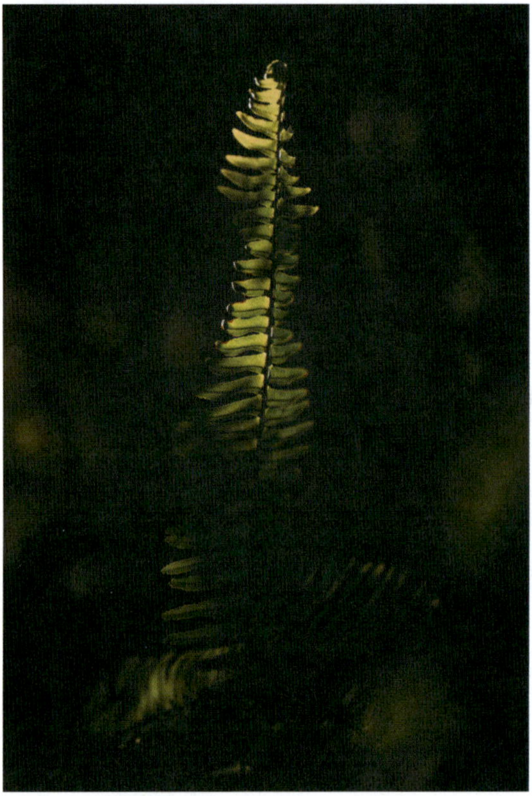

Be strong.
Be brave.
Be gentle.
Be kind.
Tolerate zero nonsense of any kind.
Listen to hear.
Speak to be understood.
Follow your heart.
Let go of the past.
Love hard.
Forgive, always forgive.
Respect yourself, or nobody else will.
Show mercy, for someday *you* may need it.
Be tolerant.
Just breathe.
Above all, just *be*, my friends, just *be*...

Made in United States
Orlando, FL
19 August 2024